A DICTIONARY OF UNIVERSALLY USED
FENCING TERMINOLOGY

William M. Gangler

A DICTIONARY OF UNIVERSALLY USED

FENCING TERMINOLOGY

WITH APPROVAL OF THE JOINT BOARD OF ACCREDITATION OF
THE UNITED STATES FENCING ASSOCIATION COACHES COLLEGE
AND THE SAN JOSÉ STATE UNIV. FENCING MASTERS PROGRAM

WILLIAM M. GAUGLER

MAESTRO DI SCHERMA
ACCADEMIA NAZIONALE DI SCHERMA, NAPLES, ITALY
HONORARY MEMBER, ASSOCIAZIONE ITALIANA MAESTRI DI SCHERMA

A LANCE C. LOBO BOOK

LAUREATE PRESS
BANGOR, MAINE

Laureate Press, Lance C. Lobo, Publisher – Telephone 800-946-2727

Original Title: Compilation of Universally Used Fencing Terminology

Manufactured in the United States of America.

 The paper used in this book meets the minimum requirements of the American National Standard for Information Services – Permanence of Paper for Printed Library Materials, ANSI Z39.48-1984.

First Edition 2 4 6 8 10 9 7 5 3 1

Library of Congress Catalog Card Number: 96-80249

Library of Congress Cataloging in Publication Data
Gaugler, William M. 1931–.
  A *Dictionary of Universally Used Fencing Terminology*
    p. cm.
  "A Lance C. Lobo Book"
  Includes bibliographical references.
  ISBN 1-884528-00-7 (alk. paper) $9.95
1. Fencing. I. Title.
GV1147   96-80249
786.8'6—dc20   CIP

Contents

Introduction
Origins of Modern Fencing Terminology

Fencing terminology has over the centuries varied from school to school and within a given school. For example, both Italian and French fencing masters employ a term derived from the same Latin root *ligare,* to bind or tie, which has become Italian *legare* and French *lier.* The difficulty is that the word, as it exists in the modern fencing vocabulary, has acquired a different meaning in each of the two languages. The Italians use the term to signify an engagement *(legamento),* while the French employ it to designate a bind *(liement).* The Germans translate the Italian word for engagement as *Bindung* or bind, while the English use the same term as the French, engagement. The matter becomes further complicated when we consider the difference between the Italo-German and Franco-English definition for engagement. For the Italians and Germans engagement means domination of the opposing steel, strong or middle against weak, while for the French and English engagement signifies blade contact alone.

Similarly, differences have resulted within the same school as the meaning of a word has changed with the passage of time. For instance, seventeenth-century Italian fencing teachers – like their modern French counterparts – refer to a circular blade action effected in time in opposition to disengagement of the opposing steel as a counter-disengagement *(contracavatione),* while their contemporary successors designate a feint by disengagement followed by a circular blade motion or deceive as a counter-disengagement *(controcavazione).* French masters, on the other hand, have had difficulty since the nineteenth century in agreeing on the definition of the terms, *redoublement* and *reprise.*

As is well known, the earliest surviving treatises on fencing were published by sixteenth-century fencing masters such as Achille Marozzo (1536), Jeronimo De Carranza (1569), Joachim Meyer (1570), and Henry De Sainct-

Didier (1573). These teachers established the theoretical foundations of the four principal sixteenth-century European schools: Italian, Spanish, German, and French.

With the dissemination of Italian Renaissance culture in the sixteenth and seventeenth centuries, all things Italian, including fencing technique, enjoyed wide popularity. The French royal family, for example, employed Italian fencing masters, such as Pompee and Silvie, while French and German teachers often traveled to Italy to study with celebrated Italian masters. The result was that Italian fencing terms entered both the French and German vocabularies. In France Italian theory was quickly modified and Italian fencing terms were assimilated and became part of the French fencing vocabulary, so that by the end of the seventeenth century a distinct French school evolved, while in Germany Italian terms in their original form, such as *filo* and *battuta,* persisted well into the twentieth century. The Spanish school, however, ceased to exist as an independent entity by the early nineteenth century. Manuel Antonio De Brea (1805), for instance, in the title of his work on swordplay indicates that he follows a mixed French, Italian, and Spanish doctrine; while Julio Castelló (1933), writing in the present century, states that he teaches his students French foil and Italian sabre.

In the sixteenth century the English, like the French, were fascinated by Italian fencing. Italian masters opened schools in England, and Italian fencing theory became popular through the publications of Giacomo di Grassi (1594) and Vincentio Saviolo (1595). Because of these influences Italian fencing terms such as *imbroccata, mandritta, riverso,* and *stoccata* entered the English vocabulary. In the century that followed, the proximity of France led to an increasing interest in French fencing methods in England. This is clearly evident in the fencing manuals of William Hope, which appeared between 1687 and 1729. However, even as late as the middle of the eighteenth century, when the French system of fencing was well established in England, Italian fencing theory continued to exert some influence on the British fencing community. This was due largely to Domenico Angelo Malevolti Tremamondo, who arrived in England in 1750, and founded a fencing academy that was to last until the end of the nineteenth century. Although originally trained in the Italian school, Domenico completed his instruction under the famous French master, Teillagory, and later wrote a treatise (1763) combining the French and Italian systems. The publication found such favor in France, as well as England, that Denis Diderot included copies of the plates in his *Encyclopedie.*

At the beginning of the nineteenth century the two dominant surviving national systems of fencing instruction were the Italian and the French. The method of each school is described in detail by the Italians, Rosaroll Scorza and Pietro Grisetti (1803), and the Frenchman, La Boëssière (1818). Examination of their treatises reveals that the Italian and French definitions and grouping of actions during the lesson generally resemble those we employ today. Except for the parries of *sixte* and *septime,* the modern French numbering system was in place. La Boëssière still advocates a guard position with the extended sword arm appropriate to duelling, and calls the parries of *sixte* and *septime,* respectively, *quarte sur les armes* and *demi-cercle,* the latter, he says is the parry used in opposition to *quarte basse.* As is obvious, these are vestigial remnants of the older Italian guard position, the parry for the outside high line with the hand in fourth position *(posizione di pugno di quarta),* the parry of half circle *(mezzocerchio),* and the thrust to low fourth *(quarta bassa).*

Modern Italian fencing theory achieved its present form by the end of the nineteenth century when Masaniello Parise's landmark publication on foil and sabre (1884) was selected by a national commission to serve as the official textbook for the Military Fencing Masters School in Rome. As first director of the school, Parise trained the majority of teachers who dominated Italian fencing during the early decades of the twentieth century. On his death in 1910, Parise was succeeded by his assistants, Salvatore Pecoraro and Carlo Pessina. Both men had been trained in the Radaellian sabre school, and now collaborated in writing a new, official sabre manual (1910). This text, along with Parise's work, provided the theoretical basis for teacher-training in Italy up to the 1970s. At that time it was decided to introduce new texts, which would incorporate the technical changes that had occurred since 1910. Giorgio Pessina and Ugo Pignotti were entrusted with the responsibility of writing these up-to-date books, one on foil (1970) and the other on sabre (1972). The companion volume on épée (1971) was initiated by Giuseppe Mangiarotti and completed by Edoardo Mangiarotti.

Jean-Louis Michel and Bertrand are generally accepted as the founders of the modern French school. Unfortunately, neither of these great fencing teachers wrote a treatise, but Arsène Vigeant (1883) records examples of Jean-Louis' lessons, and both Camille Prévost (1886) and Georges Robert (1900) have preserved Bertrand's technical method. In 1908 the new Military *Règlement* for Fencing fixed the principles of twentieth-century French fencing theory. Like Parise's work in Italy, the *Règlement* served as a guide to authors of contemporary fencing manuals, such as Pierre Thirioux (1970), Raoul Cléry (1973), and Daniel Revenu (1992).

Fencing in the United States, like England, was influenced chiefly by the French school during the nineteenth and early twentieth centuries. Teachers such as Louis Rondelle and François Darrieulat taught several generations of American fencers classical French foil technique. Rondelle (1892) left a record of his pedagogical method in a comprehensive work on foil and sabre, while Darrieulat's system of foil instruction was preserved in a small volume by his pupils, Scott Breckinridge Senior and Junior (1941). Masters from other European countries followed, bringing with them the methodology of the Spanish, Italian, Belgian, Hungarian, Polish, and Russian schools. Among those whose publications have had the most significant effect on twentieth-century American fencing methodology were Julio Castelló (1933), Aldo Nadi (1943), and Clovis Deladrier (1948).

Although sabre fencing was practiced in many European countries – usually for military purposes – modern sabre technique, based on use of a light weapon, was developed in Italy by Giuseppe Radaelli around the middle of the nineteenth century. Foil provided the foundation for Radaellian sabre theory. Radaelli's followers, Luigi Barbasetti and Carlo Pessina, carried the principles of Radaellian sabre practice to the Italian Military Fencing Masters School at Rome where they taught during the final decades of the nineteenth century.

In 1894 Barbasetti opened a fencing salle in Vienna, and the following year was asked to reorganize the Austro-Hungarian Normal Military Fencing School at Wiener-Neustadt; there he trained many of the future Austrian and Hungarian sabre teachers. Then in 1896 Italo Santelli, a pupil of Carlo Pessina and graduate of the Italian Military Fencing Masters School at Rome, was invited by the Hungarian government to teach fencing in Budapest. Since there was already a long tradition of sabre fencing in Hungary, Santelli contributed the theoretical and practical method of the Radaellian school, thus creating the Italo-Hungarian sabre method. Later, his Hungarian associates modified the system, retaining Italian fencing theory, but discarding the Italian exercises with circular cuts from the elbow, substituting in their place short cuts executed from the wrist. The most influential Hungarian teacher, recognized by many as the father of the modern Hungarian sabre school, was László Borsody, fencing master of the Toldi Miklos Royal Hungarian Sport Institute.

The success of Hungarian sabre fencers before and after the Second World War prompted fencing masters in Bulgaria, Poland, Romania, and the Soviet Union to adopt the Hungarian method. Eventually each national group modified the Hungarian pedagogical approach and, as a consequence, developed its own school. The main features they shared in common were: 1) a highly-organized program of physical training with emphasis on footwork drills, and 2) the modification of fencing actions to serve the needs of modern fencing competition.

It would also be appropriate here to note that Hungarian foil technique, although initially based on the Italian system, was modified to include French features such as eight, instead of four, parries. These changes came as a result of André Gardère's stay in Hungary during the 1930s.

The last weapon to be included in modern fencing was the épée. This was introduced into the French fencing academies during the final decades of the nineteenth century despite the objection of conservative fencing masters who regarded épée fencing as a prostitution of foil fencing. Épée technique in its formative period is described by the French teachers, Jules Jacob (1887) and Anthime Spinnewyn and Paul Manoury (1898), and by the Italian masters, Aurelio Greco (1907) and Agesilao Greco (1912). Both French and Italian teachers based their épée method, in general, on the principles of foil fencing. The absence of right of way and expanded target area distinguished épée from foil fencing. As in foil, the two dominant schools were the French and the Italian. Hungarian épée technique was derived from the Italian system through Eduardo Alajmo, who taught in the Toldi Miklos Sport Institute in Hungary during the 1930s. The Alajmo method is described in a treatise by Eduardo's brother, Michele (1936), and may also be found in its modified Hungarian form in a publication by Eduardo's pupil, Imre Vass (1976).

From the beginning of the twentieth century to the end of the Second World War German fencing was dominated by Italian masters from the Military Masters School at Rome; Ettore Schiavoni, for example, taught in Berlin, and Arturo Gazzera and Francesco Tagliabò in Frankfurt. Since the post-war period German masters have developed a German school which follows, in general, the theory of the Italian school, but has added some French features. For instance, Emil Beck at Tauberbischofsheim uses the French numbering system for parries.

In the list of fencing terms that follows, French, German, Hungarian, and Italian sources will be identified by the numbers indicated in the Bibliography. Since German and Hungarian theory is derived from French and Italian theory, repetition is avoided by citing, in many cases, only the original French and Italian sources.

Absence of blade the action of detaching one's blade from the opponent's. A fencer who does not cross swords is also said to be fencing with absence of blade.[12]

Action *(azione)* in fencing, signifies an operation in its entirety, whether offensive or defensive.[14]

Actions of concealment *(traccheggio)* *Italian.* movements used to confuse the opponent and hide one's own intentions. These consist of changes in placement of the weapon, transports, envelopments, pressures, and tight disengagements that move rapidly around the opposing steel, combined with small forward and backward steps.[16]

Actions on the blade *Italian.* movements that deviate or deflect the opposing steel during the attack; these are glides *(fili)*, blade seizure *(presa di ferro)*, changes of engagement *(cambiamenti di legamento)*, transports *(trasporti)*, envelopments *(riporti)*, beats *(battute)*, expulsions *(sforzi)*, pressures *(deviamenti)*, blade cover *(copertino)*, and disarmaments *(disarmi)*. Only the glides are performed in one motion.[16]

Advance 1. *French.* made to gain fencing measure and come close enough to the adversary so that he may be touched.[20] **2.** *French.* the action of approaching the adversary when he is not carrying out an attack.[37] **3.** *Italian.* the step forward to diminish the distance to the adversary, and to attain a fencing measure that will allow him to be hit with a lunge.[30] **4.** *Italian.* a step forward to decrease measure between oneself and the adversary. This movement is also referred to as gaining ground.[16]

Angulation 1. *French.* some extra precision may be gained when attacking the advanced target in the low line close to the bell guard, by turning the hand to full pronation. The blade is angulated upwards towards the target and permits the point to be placed with accuracy.[11] **2.** *Italian.* in épée fencing, is a thrust, effected with a flexed wrist, that passes over, under, or on either side of the adversary's bell guard to the advanced target. It may be directed to the top of the arm, bottom of the arm, internal arm, and external arm.[16]

Appel 1. *French.* to strike the ground with the right foot in a manner that produces a certain sound. The object is to attract the attention of the adversary, or to shake him up; it may be made with an advance after engagement; and it is ordinarily accompanied by a threat or another demonstration of attack to which one wishes to give a greater sense of reality.[17] **2.** *French.* to strike the earth with the foot.[20] **3.** *French.* the action of striking the ground with the right foot. Its purpose is to rattle the adversary, or, in certain cases, to reinforce the effect of a false attack. It is also employed during instruction to insure that the student's body is correctly centered over the legs in the guard position.[36] **4.** *French.* the action of striking the ground with one of the two feet. Executed with the leading foot it can shake up the adversary, or reinforce, in certain cases, the false attack. Accomplished at the end of the advance, with the rear foot, it facilitates the dynamic extension of the back leg in the lunge. It is also employed in the instruction of a beginner to insure that his weight is well distributed between the legs.[9] **5.** *Italian.* a movement the fencer makes with his right foot, raising it about two inches above the ground, and then replacing it quickly. It serves to determine correct equilibrium in the guard position; and it is often used with the feint preceding a thrust in order to entrap the adversary.[25] **6.** *Italian.* a foot stamp that may be employed to give impetus to the thrust in a renewed attack, or to accent the feint. It can also be used in the lesson as an instructional device to retard the impulse to lunge early.[16]

Appuntata (see *remise*) a counterattack used against those who habitually, after parrying the attack, riposte with a feint.[30]

Arrest 1. *French.* when the time thrust is executed on an attack made with an advance, it is called an arrest.[17] **2.** *French.* a simple attack made on the adversary's advance to arrest him as he attacks with a step forward.[33] **3.** *French.* the counterattack when it is executed (with or without a lunge) on the advance of the adversary.[36] **4.** *French.* the stop-hit (arrest) is a counteroffensive movement which must, by hitting the attacker, arrest him in the development of his attack and fulfill the implication of its name.[12] **5.** *French.* a direct counteroffensive action that steals a tempo from the offense.[42] **6.** *French.* a uniquely offensive action, designed to touch an adversary who in his attack commits a technical error – such as making feints with the point outside the target while withdrawing the arm.[9] **7.** *Hungarian.* exclusively an offensive action with the aim of stopping the adversary as he takes a step forward or attacks with a bent arm.[6] **8.** *Italian.* a counterattack that serves to interrupt, or better, to arrest completion of a compound attack. If it is opposed to a single feint it is executed in the first tempo; if it is opposed to a double feint, it can also be performed in the second tempo.[30] **9.** *Italian.* a counterattack that interrupts completion of a compound attack with feints. Attacks with a single feint are arrested on the first movement; attacks with a double feint, on either the first or second movement. When it is made on the first movement of an attack with an advance, it is generally executed with a half lunge; when it is made on the second motion, it is accomplished from the guard.[16]

Arrest in countertime an action opposed to a single or double feint in time. It is executed in the same manner as an arrest against a compound attack.[16]

Arrest with reassemblement an épée action in which the arrest to the advanced target or body is executed while withdrawing the right foot until it touches the left heel, straightening the legs, and throwing back the left arm.[16]

Ascending cut a circular cut to the flank or abdomen delivered in an ascending motion. Its function is to pass under the adversary's elbow.[16]

Assault *(assalto)* a simulated duel.[14]

Attack into the attack *French.* a thrust delivered to the adversary with a lunge at the same time that he launches his assault. These two actions sometimes seem to be simultaneous, and therefore make it difficult to discern which of the two fencers had the initiative, and was first.[9]

Attacks in time offensive actions effected while the adversary is in the act of changing the placement of his weapon. In other words, the attack is executed just as the opposing steel is moved from an invitation to an engagement or vice versa, or put in line.[16]

Attacks on the blade (see *attaques au fer*).

Attacks on the preparation *French.* actions carried out on the adversary's preparatory movements, such as when the opponent advances to close fencing measure, engages, changes engagement, doubles the engagement, invites, beats, presses or expells the weapon, tries to seize it, leans forward with his body, or when he makes a feint.[9]

Attaques au fer *French.* the group of actions that attack the opponent's blade: *battement, pression,* and *froissement.*[36]

Auxiliary actions actions that the Roman-Neapolitan school does not consider fundamental: thrust in low fourth (French *septime*), forced glides, false beats, expulsions, blade cover, change beats, beat in false fourth (French *septime*), disarmaments, renewed attacks.[30]

Azioni volanti *old Italian.* all offensive actions executed without maintaining blade contact. Among these are the straight thrust *(botta dritta),* disengagement *(cavazione),* and cut-over *(cavazione angolata).*

Balestra *Italian.* an attack executed with a jump and lunge.[27]

Beat **1.** *French.* a crisp movement of the blade against the opponent's with the object of knocking it aside or obtaining a reaction, is called a beat.[12] **2.** *Italian.* a blow of measured violence delivered with the strong of the blade against the medium of the adversary's steel to dislodge it from engagement or its position in line. The line in which the attacking blade encounters the opposing steel identifies the beat: we therefore speak of beats in first, second, third, and fourth.[16]

Beat in false fourth *Italian.* an auxiliary action executed when the adversary's weapon is held in the low line. It is performed in a horizontal direction from right to left.[30]

Beats, kinds *Italian.* simple, change, circular, and grazing.[16]

Behavior Lambertini[23] provides the following regulations concerning social behavior in the fencing room:

General Obligations

Article 1. All individuals occupying the fencing room must behave in a civil and educated manner.

Article 2. On entering, as well as leaving, it is necessary to greet everyone in the room (shake hands).

Article 3. During the lessons the bystanders must not prevent the student from hearing the master's voice.

Article 4. It is prohibited to engage in the exercise of arms in the fencing room without a protective jacket, glove, and mask appropriate to the weapon in use, in order to avoid accidents.

Obligations of the Students

Article 1. Anyone wishing to take fencing lessons must contact the master to arrange the day, hour, and monthly fee.

Article 2. Every student must provide himself with the necessary equipment for fencing; and lacking this, may not use that of other persons without their permission.

Article 3. Students may free fence only if the master, knowing their ability, gives them permission.

Article 4. It is the obligation of the students themselves, when fencing, to observe from time to time, whether or not the point of the weapon is covered with a button, so that accidents can be avoided.

Article 5. It is absolutely obligatory when fencing, that every time one is hit, to announce the touch, saying *toccato*.

Article 6. During fencing, if one of the two fencers is by chance disarmed, and his weapon drops, the other, regardless of his rank, must pick it up and hand it to his adversary by the guard, in order to avoid even the idea of haughtiness.

Article 7. If it occurs that the master breaks one or more blades in the lesson or assault, when training his students, it is their obligation to pay for the broken blades. Similarly, if not as an obligation, at least out of courtesy, it is customary that when a guest breaks his blade that his host pays for it. And when two students fence and break blades, no reason for why the blades were broken is sought; instead, the expense is always borne by the individual left holding the broken weapon.

Article 8. Smoking is not permitted in the fencing room.

Bind *(liement)* **1.** *French.* when the blades are engaged, the action of carrying the opponent's blade diagonally across from a high to a low line, or vice versa.[12] **2.** *Italian.* the movement is called a transport and glide.[16]

Blade seizure *(presa di ferro)* *Italian.* an action on the blade opposed to the adversary's weapon in line executed by first engaging the hostile steel and then adding the thrust or feint is called blade seizure.[16]

Botta (see *botte*) *Italian.* the thrust is called both *la botta* and *il colpo.*[30]

Botte (see *botta*) Labat (1696) uses the words *la botte* and *le coup* interchangeably to indicate a thrust.

Ceding or yielding parries: Foil 1. *French.* taken on the final movement of attacks executed with takings of the blade. It consists of not offering resistance to the opposition sought by the antagonist; this results in a pivoting action that rotates the point to a diagonal line opposite that in which the thrust was directed. During this motion blade contact is maintained.[9] **2.** *Hungarian.* a particular method of execution used against bind thrusts. The hand makes a funnel-like movement as the two blades remain in contact with the point of contact acting as the tip of the funnel. The blade and point begin to move in a direction opposite than in which the hand acts in executing its funnel-like action. The ceding parries are: ceding high seventh or first parry against sixth bind thrust, and ceding low fourth parry against eighth or second bind thrust.[24] **3.** *Italian.* in their execution they do not resist as do other parries; instead, they yield to the movement of the adversary's blade. The ceding parries are: the ceding parry of fourth (or inside), which is opposed to the flanconades in fourth or second, and against the glide in second; and the ceding parry of third (or outside), which is opposed to the glide in the inside low line.[32] **4.** *Italian.* the person attacked, instead of opposing the glides with counterpressure, utilizes the pressure, to some extent, by yielding from the wrist and by rotation around his opponent's blade without losing contact with it. Thus, the glide is forced from its line. There are yielding parries in first, in third, and in fourth.[3] **5.** *Italian.* used in opposition to gliding actions in the low lines. Instead of resisting the attack, it is yielded to, blades in constant contact, hand lowered, wrist flexed, and point raised, so that the parry is assumed, and the incoming steel deviated, just before the point reaches its destination. There are two ceding parries in foil fencing: the ceding parry of third, and the ceding parry of fourth. The ceding parry of third is employed against the glide in first and the internal flanconade; the ceding parry of fourth, in opposition to the glide in second, flanconade in second, and flanconade in fourth.[16]

Ceding or yielding parries: Sabre 1. *Italian.* executed in first and in low fourth against the glide in third and second. These movements are called yielding parries because they deflect the point while yielding to your adversary's pressure without losing contact with his blade.[4] **2.** *Italian.* employed against gliding actions. There are two ceding parries in sabre fencing: the ceding parry of first, and the ceding parry of fourth. These are used, respectively, in opposition to the glide in third, and the glide in second.[16]

Cercle *old French.* the parry of counter of *septime.*[37]

Change beat *Italian.* made from one's own or the adversary's engagement by carrying the point over or under the opposing steel, and striking it on the opposite side.[16]

Change of engagement 1. *French.* to change the line, passing one's weapon under the adversary's, and rejoining it in the opposite line.[10] **2.** *French.* an engagement taken in the line opposite the one in which the blade originally was.[9] **3.** *Italian.* when one shifts from an engagement to an opposite engagement, that is, from first to second and vice versa, and from third to fourth and vice versa. In the change of engagement from first to second and vice versa, the point passes over the opposing blade, and from third to fourth and vice versa, it passes under.[30] **4.** *Italian.* used to shift from one engagement to another. These movements are accomplished by passing the point over or under the opposing steel and carrying it to an opposite line of engagement. If the engagement is in the low line, the point passes over the hostile blade; if it is in the high line, it passes under.[16]

Circular beat *Italian.* executed in precisely the same manner as a circular parry: the hand remains fixed in its position of invitation or engagement, while the point, set in motion by the fingers and wrist, describes a tight, complete circle around the adversary's extended blade, beating it in the direction of the invitation or engagement.[16]

Circular cut 1. *Italian.* a rotational movement executed with the sabre to deliver a cut.[29] **2.** *Italian.* made in one movement and reaches the target via a circular route.[16]

Circular parry (see also counter-parry) **1.** *French.* a complete circle executed with the point, departing from the position in which one is on guard, and returning, after its travels, to the same position. The circular parry always takes the name of the position at its point of departure.[20] **2.** *French.* also *contre,* takes the steel from one line and carries it to the opposite line. The hand remains in place; only the fingers are used in passing the point under the adversary's blade and returning it to the initial position.[42] **3.** *Italian.* assuming the position of invitation or engagement, instead of moving the weapon to the opposite side to defend against a straight thrust or disengagement, one uses the wrist as a pivot, and describing a complete circle with the point of the weapon around the adversary's steel, the blade returns to the point of departure.[30] **4.** *Italian.* defensive blade movements in which the point describes a tight, complete circle around the incoming steel, intercepting and transferring it to the opposite line. At the completion of the action the point is in exactly the same position it was before the parry was executed.[16]

Composed attacks (compound attacks) 1. when a fencer is no longer able to touch his adversary with simple attacks, he must turn to compound attacks, that is, actions comprised of two or three movements, of which the first or the first two simulate a thrust or remove the opponent's menacing blade in line, and the last is the real thrust directed to the exposed target area.[35] **2.** offensive actions consisting of two or more blade movements. According to Italian fencing theory, compound attacks may be divided into three groups: feints, actions on the blade, and renewed attacks.[16]

Compound attacks with feints 1. *French.* those in which the simple thrust is preceded by one or more feints or an action on the blade. The compound attack should never consist of more than three feints and the thrust. We establish a complete series of compound attacks with feints up to four tempi: one-two (eludes one simple parry); one-counter-disengagement (eludes one circular parry); one-two-three (eludes two simple parries); one-two-counter-disengagement (eludes one simple and one circular parry); one-counter-disengagement-one (eludes one circular and one simple parry); one-counter-desengagement two times (eludes two circular parries); one-two-three-four (eludes three simple parries); one-two-three-counter-disengagement (eludes two simple and one circular parry), one-two-counter-disengagement-one (eludes one simple, one circular, and one simple parry); one-two-counter-disengagement two times (eludes one simple and two circular parries); one-counter-disengagement-one-two (eludes one circular and two simple parries); one-counter-disengagement in one line and one-counter-disengagement in the other (eludes one circular, one simple, and one circular), one-counter-disengagement two times-one (eludes two circular and one simple parry), one-counter-disengagement three times (eludes three circular parries). These fourteen catagories of compound attacks, in turn, yield one-hundred and sixty-eight different thrusts.[17] **2.** *French.* the action of making a false thrust, and must be so executed as to be taken for a real one. This move obliges your adversary to parry. Attacks composed of two movements are the: one-two; double; cut-over and disengage; cut-over and deceive. Attacks composed of three movements are the: one-two-three; one-two and deceive; double and disengage; cut-over and one-two. Attacks composed of four movements are the: one-two-three-four; one-two-three and deceive; one-two-deceive and disengage; double and one-two; double in both lines.[38] **3.** *French.* when the attack is preceded by one or more feints. Its function is to draw the adverse steel from one line, so that a touch may be delivered in another. When the attack is composed of a feint by disengagement to elude one simple parry, it is called, for short, a one-two; when it is comprised of two feints by disengagement to elude two simple parries it is termed a one-two-three; and when it consists of a feint by disengagement to elude a circular parry, it is designated a double.[36] **4.** *Italian.* the aim of the feint is always that of simulating an action to induce the adversary to parry, so that he may be hit where he has uncovered himself. In opposition to simple parries there are the feint direct; feint by disengagement; double feint direct; double feint by disengagement; feint by glide; double feint by glide; feint by forced glide; and double feint by forced glide. And in opposition to circular, and simple and circular parries, there are the feint direct and deceive; feint by disengagement and deceive; feint direct, deceive, and disengagement; feint by disengagement, deceive, and disengagement; double feint direct and deceive; double feint by disengagement and deceive; feint by glide and deceive; double feint by glide and deceive; feint by forced glide and deceive; and double feint by forced glide and deceive.[28] **5.** *Italian.* a movement executed with the weapon that is capable of inducing the adversary to believe that a particular fencing action will cause him damage, but which the attacker does not, in fact, intend to bring to completion. There is the feint direct and disengagement; feint by disengagement and disengagement or one-two; feint direct and deceive; feint by disengagement and deceive or double; double feint direct and disengagement; double feint by disengagement and disengagement or one-two-three; double feint direct and deceive; double feint by disengagement and deceive or one-two-deceive; feint direct, deceive, and disengagement; feint by disengagement, deceive, and disengagement or double feint and disengagement; double feint direct, deceive, and disengagement; double feint by disengagement, deceive, and disengagement or one-two, deceive, and disengagement; feint direct, deceive, disengagement, and deceive; and feint by disengagement, deceive, disengagement, deceive or counter-disengagement in the two opposing lines; feint by glide and disengagement; double feint by glide and disengagement; feint by glide and deceive; and double feint by glide and deceive.[32] **6.** *Italian.* a simulated thrust or menace that resembles so closely a genuine assault that the adversary is forced to parry. In contrast to a real attack, it does not end in a lunge or running attack. The compound attacks with feints are the feint direct and disengagement; feint by disengagement and disengagement; feint by glide and disengagement (eluding one simple parry); double feint direct and disengagement; double feint by disengagement and disengagement; double feint by glide and disengagement (eluding two simple parries); feint direct and deceive; feint by disengagement and deceive; feint by glide and deceive (eluding one circular parry); feint direct, deceive, and disengagement; feint by disengagement, deceive, and disengagement; feint by glide, deceive, and disengagement (eluding one circular and one simple parry); double feint direct and deceive; double feint by disengagement and deceive; double feint by glide and deceive (eluding one simple and one circular parry); feint direct and double deceive; feint by disengagement and double deceive; feint by glide and double deceive (eluding two circular parries); double feint direct, deceive, and disengagement; double feint by disengagement, deceive, and disengagement; double feint by glide, deceive and disengagement (eluding one simple, one circular, and one simple parry); feint direct, deceive, disengagement, and deceive; feint by disengagement, deceive, disengagement, and deceive; feint by glide, deceive, disengagement, and deceive (eluding one circular, one simple, and one circular parry); feint direct and cut-over; feint by disengagement and cut-over; feint by glide and cut-over (eluding one simple parry); and feint by cut-over and disengagement (eluding one simple parry). All compound feint attacks with the point in line can be executed in opposition to the four invitations and engagements. Compound attacks with the cut-over, however, can only be performed in opposition to engagements in third and fourth.[16]

Compound ripostes 1. *French.* those that are preceded by one or more feints: one-two, double, cut-over-disengage, etc.[9] **2.** *Hungarian.* one or more feints.[6] **3.** *Italian.* ripostes consisting of two or more blade motions; their function is to elude one or more counterparries, that is, parries opposed to the riposte.[16]

Contraries 1. *Italian.* all those movements that are developed to destroy the adversary's actions.[39] **2.** *Italian.* for every action in fencing there is a counteraction.[16]

Contre-degagement according to La Boëssière, consists of disengaging two times in the same direction, and for this reason it is also called the *double-degagement.*[8]

Contre-temps (see countertime).

Contro-cavazione Florio[15], following the oldest Italian tradition, states that the *contro-cavazione* is a circle made in the same direction as that of the adversary, but he prefers to call this action a *concavazione.* Pessina and Pignotti[30] designate a feint by disengagement and deceive *(finta di cavazione circolata)* as a *controcavazione.*

Conventional exercises 1. *German.* in these exercises (conventional – because they are established by mutual consent) offensive as well as defensive actions are agreed upon. Even though these drills reflect competitive situations, their measure and time are fixed.[21] **2.** *Italian.* consist of pre-establishing, between two fencers, actions that each of them must execute relative to offense and defense, paying scrupulous attention, during alternate execution of the actions, how they were set up. These exercises integrate in an excellent way the benefits of the lesson and constitute above all the first steps of a free application of offense and relative defense.[30] **3.** *Italian.* consist of pre-established actions executed by two fencers alternately assuming the role of attacker and defender. The purpose is to perfect the various offensive and defensive movements studied in the lesson, and to develop, through practice, a sense of fencing measure and time.[16]

Coulé (see glide, graze, and *filo*).

Counter-disengagement (see *contre-degagement* and *contro-cavazione*) Clèry[9] includes the counter-disengagement among the simple attacks and says that it is a disengagement that serves to avoid completion of adverse engagements and single and double changes of engagement. Bay, Rerich, and Tilli[6] state that it is a circular action in time employed against the adversary's single and double changes of engagement. It can also be classified as an action in time used in opposition to the adversary who repeatedly frees his blade from engagement, or disengages in time to avoid contact.[16]

Counter-parry (see circular parry).

Counterparry riposte (see counter-riposte) *Italian.* the parry and riposte that follow the initial parry and riposte; in other words, after the attack has been parried the riposte may be opposed with the counterparry riposte.[16]

Counter-riposte (see counterparry riposte) **1.** *French.* the offensive movement which follows a successful parry of a riposte. It can be delivered by either the attacker or the defender, and can be simple or compound.[12] **2.** *French.* the thrust delivered after the adverse riposte has been parried.[9] **3.** *Hungarian.* the riposte that follows the parry of the opponent's riposte.[6]

Countertime 1. *French.* the action of drawing the opponent's arrest (stop-hit) or time thrust (time-hit), parrying it, and riposting from it.[12] **2.** *French.* a tactic that consists of provoking an offensive or counteroffensive reaction so that this can be opposed with a riposte or attack. Movements that will draw an attack or counterattack are the advance, forward motion of the body, feint, false attack, invitation, and action on the blade.[9] **3.** *Italian.* movements used in opposition to counterattacks. They are simulated attacks designed to provoke the opponent's counterthrusts, thus exposing him to a parry and riposte, or to the counterattack into the counterattack. The initial motion of the action must be sufficiently clear to induce the adversary to counterattack, without being so obvious that he suspects a trap. This can be accomplished by combining an accented feint or attack on the blade with an advance. The feint direct, feint by disengagement, or simple beat, executed with a step forward, provide excellent bait for the counterattacker.[16]

Covering *French.* to engage in such a way that the line in which the swords are crossed is closed to a straight thrust.[12]

Croisé 1. *French.* an action that carries the opponent's blade from high to low line on the same side as the engagement and does not, as in the bind, carry it diagonally across. It is not executed from low to high line.[12] **2.** *Italian.* the *croisé* ending in the outside low line or flank is called the *fianconata esterna* (external flanconade) or *fianconata di quarta* (flanconade in fourth). **3.** *old French.* Labat (1696), for example, also called this action *la flanconade.*

Cut-over 1. *French.* to go from one high line to the other there is a way other than by disengagement, and it consists of passing the point of the weapon over that of the adversary.[17] **2.** *French.* a disengagement that passes over the point of the adversary's weapon, instead of passing under, as in the disengagement.[10] **3.** *French.* may be considered to be like a disengagement, with the difference being that it is executed by passing the point over that of the adversary, while in the disengagement it passes under.[33] **4.** *German.* disengagement may be effected by passing under the bell guard (disengagement) or over the point (cut-over) of the opponent's weapon.[5] **5.** *Hungarian.* the point of our weapon passes over that of the adversary into another line.[6] **6.** *Italian.* a disengagement that passes over the adversary's blade in the lines of fourth and third.[32] **7.** *Italian.* a disengagement over the blade; it is an indirect attack executed in one movement, and may be used when the adversary engages in third or fourth. It can be directed to the inside and outside high lines, and to the outside low line.[16]

Deceive the counter-disengagement preceded by a feint. The two terms, "counter-disengagement" and "deceive," are interchangeable in English fencing terminology.[16]

Defense 1. *French.* in fencing, that part of the game which consists of a variety of strokes used for warding off offensive actions. To each offensive stroke there is at least one defensive action; generally, the fencer has a choice of several.[12] **2.** *Italian.* blade motions that deviate the adversary's point before it reaches the target, or foot movements that remove the body from the range of attack. The first of these is designated the defense of steel, the second, the defense of measure. In the defense of steel the offensive response can be immediate; in the defense of measure it is always delayed, thus prolonging the encounter. From this it may be surmised that the defense of steel is the more efficient of the two.[16]

Degrees or strength of the blade 1. the degrees of the blade are determined by imagining the length of the blade divided into three equal parts, the strong, which is near the bell guard, the weak, which is near the point, and the medium comprising the section between the other two.[30] **2.** divide the blade into six parts: the double strong, the strong, the less strong, the less weak, the weak, and the double weak.[40]

Demi-cercle (see *mezzo-cerchio*) *old French.* parry of half circle. In 1900 Robert[37] stated that it was necessary to suppress the use of certain fencing terms that had become out-dated. He cited as examples *demi-cercle* and *cercle,* which were once employed to designate, respectively, the parries of *septime* and counter of *septime*.

Demi-volte (also see inquartata) Angelo, in his *School of Fencing* (1787), defines the demi-volte as the half round, or bounding turn of the body.

Dérobement *French.* the disengagement in time, the counteroffensive movement which is employed in opposition to actions on the blade. The *Règlement*[36] states that *dérober* is to remove the blade from an adverse offensive action. Crosnier[12] says that a *dérobement* is an evasion. In fencing it is a term used to describe the evasion of the opponent's attempt to take, or attack, the blade.

Descending cut *(fendente)* **1.** *Hungarian.* in executing a thrown or angular cut, the fencer must round the opponent's blade by passing over its point. Angular cuts are effective only against third and fourth engagements.[24] **2.** *Italian.* executed, in one movement, from the adversary's engagements in third and fourth, raising the point, and turning the hand to third position, flexing the arm, passing the blade over that of the adversary, and directing a vertical cut to the head.[29] **3.** *Italian.* cuts made in one motion and reach the target by passing over the point of the opposing steel. From the adversary's engagement in third and fourth the hand is rotated to third position, elbow flexed, and the point passed over the hostile blade; the arm is extended, and a vertical cut delivered to the top of the head.[16]

Direct cut 1. *Hungarian.* regardless of the distance traveled by the blade or the arc it describes during the cutting action, the cut is considered as straight if the blade moves from its starting position to the target without encountering any obstructions. There are direct cuts to the head, flank, outside cheek, and chest.[24] **2.** *Italian.* made in one motion and reaches the target via the shortest route. There are direct cuts to the head, right cheek, left cheek, chest, abdomen, and flank. Cuts to the head, right cheek, and flank are pushed forward across the target in a slicing action. Cuts to the left cheek, chest, and abdomen are pulled back across the target with the hand progressively rotated, and the elbow flexed in coordination, so that the weapon, hand, and arm are returned in one continuous motion to the guard in third.[16]

Direct point thrust 1. *Hungarian.* can be executed from every fundamental position, most frequently from third, second, or possibly fifth. From first and fourth we rarely use it. At the completion of the action the arm and the blade should form an obtuse angle.[7] **2.** *Italian.* an action, without blade contact, in which the point of the sabre follows a straight line to the exposed target; it is a direct attack in one movement, and may be used in opposition to the adversary's invitations. Care should be taken that the arm and blade form an obtuse angle, so that the external arm is well protected.[16]

Disarmaments violent attacks on the opposing steel to disarm the adversary, or to make him lose control of his weapon, so that he is no longer able to defend himself. There are three disarmaments, one vertical; and two spiral, one to the left, and one to the right.[16]

Disengagement: Foil 1. *French.* the action of passing the point of the weapon from one line to another to direct it to the body.[17] **2.** *French.* the action of leaving the line where one is and thrusting in another.[33] **3.** *French.* when the point of the arm is transferred from one line to another following the shortest route.[36] **4.** *French.* a semicircular movement of the point which detaches it from the opposing steel and carries it to a neighboring line of the one just left.[9] **5.** *German.* the point of the blade, by means of a spiral-shaped movement, and with simultaneous extension of the arm, passes around the opponent's bell guard, hand, and forearm.[5] **6.** *Hungarian.* movement from a lower to a higher line effected with a half-circular motion of the point of the blade.[6] **7.** *Italian.* the action of freeing one's own blade, when it is subject to the adversary's engagement, and making the point describe a spiral in the direction of the exposed target area.[32] **8.** *Italian.* the action of detaching one's own blade from the adversary's engagement.[30] **9.** *Italian.* an action in which the blade, with a spiral motion of the point, is detached from the adversary's engagement, and directed to the exposed target; it is an indirect attack in one movement, and may be employed when the opponent engages blades.[16]

Disengagement with the point: Sabre **1.** *Hungarian.* if the opponent attempts to cover his target with an engagement of the fencer's blade, a thrust can be executed by disengaging under his blade.[24] **2.** *Italian.* an action in which the blade, with a spiral motion of the point, is detached from the opponent's engagement, and is directed to the exposed target; it is an indirect attack in one movement, and may be employed when the adversary engages blades.[16]

Disordinata *Italian.* multiple feints.[28]

Dominating the blade *(dominare o guadagnare i gradi)* placing the strong of one's own blade on the weak of the adversary's steel.[14]

Double change of engagement **1.** *French.* the immediate succession of two engagements, with the hand remaining in the same line.[9] **2.** *Italian.* the opponent's steel is carried to an opposite line, and then back again to the original line of engagement. Double changes may be effected from first to second to first, second to first to second, third to fourth to third, and fourth to third to fourth. Double changes of engagement are designated by the line of engagement in which they begin and end.[16]

Double engagement (see double change of engagement).

Double feint double feints elude two parries; they are employed in opposition to the invitation and engagement. Each feint is named after its initial movement: we therefore speak of the double feint direct, double feint by disengagement, and the double feint by glide. When the double feint is coordinated with an advance, the two feints are completed with the step forward. The first feint should coincide with the motion of the right foot, the second with the movement of the left foot, and the final thrust with the lunge.[16]

Double-feinte (see double feint) the term *double-feinte* was used by French masters in the past. Labat (1696), for example, states that it is an action executed in three movements.

Doublement *French.* a compound attack with a feint by disengagement to deceive a circular parry.[36]

Elevation of the hand 1. *French.* the first reason for elevating the hand during the attack is to facilitate reaching the adversary's body by overcoming the obstacle presented by his hand. And the second reason is to close the line by forming opposition on the side of the hostile steel to avoid a double hit.[17] **2.** *Italian.* raising the armed hand to the height of the right eye at the moment the thrust is executed. It serves as protection against a thrust the adversary can make, and also to bring, with greater facility, the point of the weapon to the opponent's chest.[14] **3.** *Italian.* in delivering the thrust major emphasis must be placed on opposition and elevation of the hand, because these represent the most effective means of impeding the adversary's thrusts along the same line.[32]

Engagement: Foil 1. *French.* the junction of two blades.[20] **2.** *French.* one is engaged in fourth when the weapons are joined in the inside line of the body; one is engaged in third when the arms are joined in the outside, that is to say, to the right of the person holding the weapon. One speaks of taking the engagement if the side is covered where one is engaged.[10] **3.** *French.* when a fencer crosses swords with his adversary. This corresponds to the line in which the swords are crossed.[12] **4.** *French.* the action of joining the adverse blade. It is also called the situation of the two blades in contact.[9] **5.** *German.* the domination of the opponent's weak blade portion with the strong of one's own blade. The opposing point must be forced out of the threatening line of offense.[21] **6.** *Italian.* that point of contact between the two opposing blades when one wants to dominate the other. To execute it properly at lunging distance, it is necessary to place the strong of one's blade on the weak of the adversary's; and from walking distance, instead of the strong, the medium. There are four engagements: fourth, which exposes the outside chest; third, which exposes the inside chest; second, which exposes the entire chest; and half circle, which exposes only the flank. These four engagements have the same purpose as the invitations, are executed with the same hand positions, and expose the same target areas.[28] **7.** *Italian.* the contact one establishes between the two blades in a way that one's own dominates that of the adversary, deviating it from the line of offense. Like the invitations, there are four engagements, and they take the same names: first or half circle, second, third, and fourth.[30] **8.** *Italian.* a contact invitation in which the opposing steel is dominated and deviated from the line of offense. There are four engagements: first, second, third, and fourth. In these the hand and weapon assume exactly the same position they did in invitations. Engagements are effected with the strong against the weak, if taken at correct or lunging distance; and with the medium against the weak, if made from out of distance [16]

Engagement: Sabre *Italian.* there are five: first, second, third, fourth, and fifth. In modern sabre fencing engagements are generally effected only in second and third.[16]

Envelopments **1.** *French.* the action of taking the weak of the opposing blade in the strong of one's own and, by describing a circle with both blades in contact, returning to the line of engagement.[12] **2.** *Italian.* movements that encircle the opposing steel, so that the blade, in continous motion and without a loss of contact, returns to the original line of engagement. They may be accomplished in all lines, and are designated by the line of engagement in which they begin and end.[16]

Esquives *French.* arrests executed while removing the target area. There are three kinds: arrest with reassemblement, inquartata, and passata sotto. Cléry[9] states that the two latter actions are no longer employed because of the risks they present.

Expulsions **1.** *French.* *(froissement)* the action of grazing the opponent's blade very strongly and sharply by bringing the strong of one's own blade diagonally down from the weak to the medium of his blade, thus deflecting it sharply.[12] **2.** *Italian.* powerful sliding beats in which the strong of the attacking weapon is forced along the opposing steel, expelling it from its position in engagement or line. They can be effected in any of the four lines, but are most commonly used in third and fourth.[16]

External flanconade *Italian.* (also flanconade in fourth) a glide to the adversary's flank, with the hand in fourth position, and opposition to the inside.[16]

False attack (see probing actions) *French.* a simple or compound attack, more or less pronounced, and in any case not completely developed, to discover the adversary's plans, or his preferred parries, so that these may be countered.[9]

False beat *Italian.* when the adversary has engaged blades and a beat is executed.[16]

Fausse attaque (see false attack).

Feint in time *Italian.* a movement opposed to actions in countertime. It is a feigned arrest or disengagement in time intended to provoke the adversary's action in countertime, so that this may be opposed with a disengagement or deceive in time.[16]

Feints 1. *French.* a simulated thrust. It is a way of drawing the opponent's blade to one line, by means of a false demonstration of attack, so that he may be hit in another.[17] **2.** *French.* simulated attacks.[33] **3.** *Italian.* every movement of the weapon not followed by a lunge, but effected to induce the adversary to parry, is called a feint. The feint, therefore, is nothing other than a simulated thrust or menace.[30] **4.** *Italian.* a simulated thrust or menace that resembles so closely a genuine assault that the adversary is forced to parry. In contrast to a real attack, it does not end in a lunge or running attack.[16]

Fencing the science and art of handling the sword.[15]

Fencing line (also see line of direction) **1.** *German.* an imagined line between two fencers that runs through their heels and the toes of the leading foot. On this line fencers move forward and backward.[21] **2.** *Hungarian.* the imaginary straight line that passes through the heels of two fencers standing opposite one another.[6] **3.** *Hungarian.* an imaginary straight line that would connect the four heels of two fencers as they face each other.[7] **4.** *Hungarian.* the imaginary line which joins the heels of the two fencers facing each other.[24]

Fendente (see descending cut) *Italian.* a cut-over or descending cut in sabre.[16]

Filo (see *coulé,* glide, and graze) *Italian.* glide.[30]

First intention when a given movement is executed with the intent of reaching the target directly through the action itself.[16]

First position 1. *French.* the feet are at right angles, with the point of the right foot opposite that of the adversary (for right-handed fencers), heels together, right before the left, legs extended, body upright, back straight, left arm falling naturally along the left thigh, hand open, fingers extended, left shoulder hidden from the adversary by profiling the body and offering as little surface as possible, head high, face turned to the adversary, right arm extended high, a little to the right of the body, and forming with the right shoulder an angle of about forty degrees, hand turned with the fingernails up, and the blade serving as a prolongation of the arm.[37]
2. *Italian.* the posture assumed by the fencer with his body and weapon before the salute and during periods of rest; the body is held erect, head up, eyes fixed on the adversary, shoulders down and level, legs together, feet at right angles, heels touching, and right toe pointing at the opponent; the armed right hand is placed against the body, a little below the belt, with the blade directed diagonally toward the ground, as though ready to be drawn from its sheath, while the left hand rests on the hip, fingers in front, and thumb behind.[16]

Flanconade in fourth (see external flanconade) *Italian.* called in modern French fencing terminology a *croisé* in fourth.[9]

Flanconade in second *Italian.* the transport to second (from engagement in fourth) and glide to the outside low line.[16]

Flanconades 1. they terminate in the flank. **2.** *Italian.* there are three flanconades: the flanconade in fourth or external flanconade, which is executed with one blade motion, and the internal flanconade and flanconade in second, which are performed with two blade movements.[16]

Flanconnade (see external flanconade or flanconade in fourth) a bind beginning in the line of fourth, and directing the thrust in the same line, but lower, while dominating the weak of the adversary's blade. It is not effected, Grisier says, as is generally believed, by carrying the blade to the line of eighth.[20]

Flèche (see running attack) **1.** *French.* the running attack. **2.** a running attack executed following a loss of balance by an exaggerated forward displacement of the center of gravity.[9]

Forced glide *(filo sottomesso)* *Italian.* a glide in opposition to the adversary's imperfect or weak engagement is called a forced glide. Its purpose is to regain opposition.[16]

Frecciata (see running attack) *Italian.* the running attack. It is a combination of movements that project the fencer forward, passing from the guard to a position in which the body is inclined decisively forward, along with the weapon arm, while the rear arm is extended backwards.[30]

Froissement (see expulsion).

Fundamental elements of fencing time, velocity, and measure.[29]

Gaining on the lunge 1. *French.* this may be used when the enemy is out of distance, or when he is known to retreat habitually upon being attacked. It consists of drawing the left foot up toward the right, the distance wished to be gained, just before lunging.[38] **2.** *Italian.* another method for closing distance. This is accomplished by drawing the left foot forward until the left heel touches the right heel and then lunging. The ground covered in this way may be equal to, or even greater, than that obtained by means of the advance lunge.[16]

Gaining measure (see gaining on the lunge) *French.* bringing the left foot close to the right to approach and attack. It is preferable to advance because one risks losing balance in the execution of this movement.[33]

Glide (see *coulé* and *filo*) **1.** *French.* the action of gliding along the adverse blade, keeping it in opposition.[38] **2.** *French.* the action of sliding with the blade along the adverse steel, extending the arm, as preparation, or for completion of the attack.[36] **3.** *Italian.* an action that from its beginning to its end is executed maintaining contact with the adverse steel.[28] **4.** *Italian.* an offensive action that one executes from one's own engagement or on the adversary's weapon in line.[30] **5.** *Italian.* an action in which the blade slides along the opposing steel to the exposed target; it is an attack in one movement that may be used when the adversary's blade is engaged.[16]

Glide with the point (sabre) *Italian.* *(filo)* an action in which the blade slides along the opposing steel to the exposed target; it is an attack in one movement that may be used when the adversary's blade is engaged in second or third.[16]

Graze (see glide, *coulé,* and *filo*) another word for glide.[12]

Grazing beat *Italian.* a sliding beat in which the point is withdrawn, and the line changed by passing over the opposing steel.[16]

Guard position 1. *French.* the unique position that permits the fencer to be equally ready for offense and defense.[36] **2.** *French.* an ideal position of equilibrium, correct for each fencer, which permits him to be ready to execute at all times, and in the briefest moment, all actions and body movements necessary for fencing.[9] **3.** *Italian.* the special position taken by the fencer with his weapon and body to attack advantageously his adversary, and to defend himself easily against attacks.[32] **4.** *Italian.* the position that is assumed by the fencer with his body and weapon to be ready for offense, defense, and counteroffense.[30]

Hand positions: Foil 1. *French.* turning the fist refers to the different positions the hand takes in turning the fingernails toward the earth or toward the sky. This results in two distinct positions: pronation and supination. Pronation is the state in which the fingernails are turned toward the earth, and supination when they are turned toward the sky. Each of these positions admits two degrees: complete pronation and partial pronation; complete supination and partial supination. In these partial states the hand does not accomplish its complete rotation, that is to say, the fingernails have made only half the turn between earth and sky. Generally, engagements, feints, and parries are made with partial supination, while complete pronation and supination are employed for the thrust. To say that the hand is in fourth when the fingernails are turned toward the sky, or in third when they are turned toward the earth is an error.[17] **2.** *French.* the hand may be placed in a number of positions between two extremes: one is obtained when the fingernails are turned completely upward, and the other, when the fingernails are turned to the right, with the thumb below. On the other hand, the blade may have, in rapport to the hand, the following positions: the point can be higher than the hand, at the height of the hand, or lower than the hand. The combinations of the diverse positions of the hand and blade constitute the fencing positions that serve as the basis for the parries. There are eight positions and they are situated in different lines. In each of the four lines two positions of the hand are utilized: one with the hand in supination, and the other with the hand in pronation. Thus, one finds third *(tierce)* and sixth *(sixte)* in the high line; fourth *(quarte)* and fifth *(quinte)* in the inside line; second *(seconde)* and eighth *(octave)* in the outside line; and first *(prime)* and seventh *(septime)* in the low line.[9] **3.** *Hungarian.* parries can be either supine or prone, depending on the position of the fencer's hand. The following parries are determined by hand position and their location: fourth (or fifth), sixth (or third), eighth (or second), seventh (or first). These parries are identical in terms of location, but differ in hand position. Those in parentheses are held in a prone hand position.[24] **4.** *Italian.* the positions of the fist may be distinguished as principal and collateral or medium – the latter are so-named because they rest between two principal positions. There are four principal positions. With the sword in hand, if the knuckle guard is turned toward the sky, the fist is said to be in first position; if the knuckle guard is rotated outside, to your right, it is in second position; if it is turned toward the earth, it is in third position; and if it is rotated toward the left, or toward your chest, it is in fourth position. There are four collateral or medium positions, and these take the names of the two principal positions on either side. Therefore, the medium position between first and second is called first in second, and so successively, second in third, third in fourth, and first in fourth.[40] **5.** *Italian.* the diverse positions the armed hand of the fencer may take are called positions of the fist; these are obtained by rotating the hand. In foil fencing there are four normal and two intermediate positions: first, second, third, fourth, second in third, and third in fourth. First is when the back of the hand faces to the left and the crossbar is perfectly vertical; second is when the back of the hand faces upward and the crossbar is horizontal; third is when the back of the hand faces right and the crossbar is vertical; fourth is when the back of the hand faces down and the crossbar is horizontal; second in third is when the fist is in an intermediate position between second and third, with the crossbar in a diagonal line to the right; third in fourth is when the fist is in an intermediate position between third and fourth, and the crossbar is in a diagonal line to the left. In foil fencing the position of the hand in first is only theoretical; the other five positions, however, all have a practical purpose in the execution of the various fencing movements.[30] **6.** *Italian.* in foil fencing there are six hand positions. Four of these are designated principal positions, and two, intermediate positions. The principal positions are first, second, third, and fourth. With the weapon in hand, the positions are obtained by rotating the hand one quarter turn for the principal positions, and one eighth turn for the intermediate positions. In first position the back of the hand faces left, crossbar vertical; in second position the back of the hand faces up, crossbar horizontal; in third position the back of the hand faces right, crossbar vertical; in fourth position the back of the hand faces down, crossbar horizontal; in second in third position the back of the hand faces obliquely up toward the right, crossbar diagonal; and in third in fourth position the back of the hand faces obliquely down toward the right, crossbar diagonal.[16]

Hand positions: Sabre *Italian.* there are seven hand positions. Four of these are termed principal positions, and three, intermediate positions. The principal positions are first, second, third, fourth; and the intermediate positions, first in second, second in third, and third in fourth. With the weapon in hand, positions are effected by rotating the hand one quarter turn for the principal positions, and one eighth turn for the intermediate positions. In first position the back of the hand faces left, cutting edge of the blade up; in second position the back of the hand faces up, cutting edge of the blade to the right; in third position the back of the hand faces right, cutting edge of the blade down; in fourth position the back of the hand faces down, cutting edge of the blade to the left; in first in second position the back of the hand faces obliquely up toward the left, cutting edge of the blade diagonal and up toward the right; in second in third position the back of the hand faces obliquely up toward the right, cutting edge of the blade diagonal and down toward the right; and in third in fourth position the back of the hand faces obliquely down toward the right, cutting edge of the blade diagonal and down toward the left.[16]

Hand positions for parries: Foil **1.** *French.* the parries of first, second, third, and fifth are taken with the hand in pronation; and the parries of fourth, sixth, seventh, and eighth are taken with the hand in supination.[33] **2.** *Italian.* in the parry of first or half circle the hand is in third in fourth position; in the parry of second the hand is in fourth or second position; in the parry of third the hand is in fourth or second in third position; and in the parry of fourth the hand is in third in fourth position.[16]

Hand positions for parries: Sabre *Italian.* in the parry of first the hand is in first position; in the parry of second the hand is in first in second position; in the parry of third the hand is in second in third position; in the parry of fourth the hand is in third in fourth position; and in the parries of fifth and sixth the hand is in first position.[16]

Imbroccata *Italian.* a counterattack against gliding attacks and ripostes that end in the outside low line, that is, the external flanconade, and the flanconade in second. The action is effected from the guard position with the hand in fourth or second position. As the adversary is in the act of completing his attack or riposte, a counterthrust, with opposition to the right, is directed along the incoming steel to the outside low line.[16]

In-fighting scoring a touch at close range before the director calls a halt to the action is termed "in-fighting." In this mode of fighting the fencer generally maintains a low guard position and concentrates on offensive actions.[27]

Initiative for the attack attacks may be executed on one's own initiative, or on the adversary's. In the first instance it is one's own selection of time that determines the moment of the assault; in the second, it is the opponent's movement of his weapon that prompts the attack.[16]

Inquartata a counterattack in opposition to both simple and compound attacks terminating in the inside high line. From an invitation or engagement in third (French *sixte*), the attack with a straight thrust or disengagement to the inside high line is opposed with the counterthrust to the same line, hand in fourth position (supination), opposition to the left, left leg extended backward, as in a lunge, and left foot shifted approximately forty-five degrees to the right of the line of direction. In opposition to a compound attack, the counterattack follows a parry.[16]

Internal flanconade *Italian.* the transport to first (from engagement in third) and glide to the inside low line.[16]

Invitations: Foil 1. *Hungarian.* the invitation and parry positions are identical hand positions. The invitation exposes the fencer's target. It actually invites the opponent to attack.[24] **2.** *Italian.* a placement taken with the weapon with the purpose of exposing a target area. There are four invitations, and they are designated: first or half circle, second, third, and fourth. The invitation of first or half circle exposes the flank or low line; the invitation of second, the chest or high line; the invitation of third, the internal chest; and the invitation of fourth, the external chest.[30] **3.** *Italian.* positions taken with the weapon, exposing a specific line, to induce the opponent to attack. There are four foil invitations: first, second, third, and fourth. The invitation in first uncovers the flank or outside low line; the invitation in second, the chest or high line; the invitation in third, the chest or inside high line; and the invitation in fourth, the chest or outside high line.[16]

Invitations: Sabre *Italian.* there are five: first, second, third, fourth, and fifth. The invitation in first exposes the flank; the invitation in second, the right or outside cheek; the invitation in third, the abdomen and left or inside cheek; the invitation in fourth, the right or outside cheek; and the invitation in fifth, the flank and abdomen.[16]

Line of direction (also see fencing line) **1.** *Italian.* an imaginary line which two fencers, in their opposing actions, must constantly maintain. The line departs from the left heel of one of the fencers, passes through the right foot of each, and terminates in the left heel of the other fencer.[32] **2.** *Italian.* the imaginary line connecting two fencers, beginning at the left heel of one, passing through the axis of his right foot, and continuing until it encounters the same points in his adversary's feet. This is the normal route the feet must travel in the lesson, in exercise, and in combat.[16]

Line of offense when the point of the weapon, with the arm naturally extended, menaces some part of the valid target area.[30]

Lines 1. *French.* the space on each side of the weapon in which one executes engagements, thrusts, attacks on the weapon, feints, and parries. The two principal lines are on the right and left sides of the weapon; those on the right are called outside, and those on the left are called inside. Each of the lines is bisected by two other lines above and below the weapon, called above and below or high and low.[17] **2.** *French.* the space comprised between one side and the other of the weapon and the limit of the body. There are four known lines in fencing: two high and two low, the weapon being placed with the point directed high or low. The four lines are inside and above for the high lines, and below and outside for the low lines. The inside line is to the left of the blade of the fencer, with the point directed high. The line above is to the right of the blade of the fencer, with the point directed high. The line below is to the left of the blade of the fencer, with the point directed low. And the line to the outside is to the right of the fencer, with the point directed low.[33] **3.** *French.* the portions of space – considered in rapport to the fencer's hand – in which the fencer is able to move his weapon. One distinguishes the high line, low line, right line, and left line.[36] **4.** *Italian.* the valid target is divided into four distinct sectors designated: internal, external, above, and below. The line traveled by the point of the weapon, when it is directed to these areas, is also called the internal, external, high, and low line.[30] **5.** *Italian.* to describe the lines of attack the adversary's body is divided into four quarters: inside, outside, high, and low. When the opponent is in the correct guard position all assaults will pass to the right or left of his sword arm, or above or below it. An attack to the right of the arm is said to enter the outside line; to the left of the arm, the inside line; above the arm, the high line; and below the arm, the low line.[16]

Lunge 1. *French.* an auxiliary movement of attack that provides the most advantageous extension of the arms and legs for the execution of the thrust.[37] **2.** *French.* (development) a combination of arm and leg movements used in fencing as a method of delivering the attack. It is composed of the extension of the sword arm, which identifies the attacker, and is followed by a lunge which is the action of the legs permitting the fencer to reach his opponent.[12] **3.** *Italian.* the movement forward of the right leg and body which the fencer makes while executing a thrust, so that he may strike his adversary from the greatest distance possible.[34] **4.** *Italian.* the position taken with the body and weapon that provides maximum force in delivering the thrust, and allows the fencer to attain the greatest reach with his body.[32] **5.** *Italian.* the fencer assumes with his body at the end of an offensive action executed from the guard. The passage from guard to lunge must be effected in a single movement.[16]

Measure: Foil 1. *French.* the correct distance for a fencer to await his adversary, and from which he may lunge. Measure varies according to the height and body type of the fencer. Between two fencers of uneqal height the advantage is with the taller, provided he keeps his adversary at a distance; but the advantage shifts to the smaller, if he is in close.[17] **2.** *French.* the greatest distance from which a fencer can reach his adversary with a lunge.[36] **3.** *German.* the distance between two adversaries. There are various measures: in tight or near measure the opponent can be hit by simply extending the arm; in middle or fixed measure the arm is extended with a step forward or lunge to score a hit; and in wide measure the arm is extended with a step forward and lunge to score a touch.[21] **4.** *Hungarian.* the greatest distance from which a fencer can reach his adversary with a lunge.[6] **5.** *Italian.* the distance between two fencers on guard, facing one another. The distances are called correct measure or lunge measure, walking measure, and close measure. One is in correct measure when it is possible to reach the adversary's target with only a lunge, in walking measure when it is possible to reach correct measure by taking at least one step forward, and in close measure when it is possible to reach the adversary without lunging.[30]

Measure: Sabre 1. *Hungarian.* we differentiate between short (closed), middle, and long fencing distance. From short distance we reach our opponent's body with our sabre by one arm movement. From middle distance we reach our opponent by one step (leap) or lunge, and one arm movement. From long distance we reach our opponent by one step (leap), one lunge, and one arm movement.[7] **2.** *Italian.* the distance between two fencers facing one another on guard. The three distances are called, respectively, correct measure or lunge measure, walking or marching measure, and close measure. From correct measure one is able to touch the adversary's body with a lunge, or to the arm while remaining in the guard position; from walking measure one is able to touch the adversary's body with a step forward and lunge, or his arm with a lunge; and from close measure one is able to touch every part of the adversary's valid target area without lunging.[31] **3.** *Italian.* the distance that separates two fencers placed on guard. There are three measures: out of distance, correct distance, and close distance. From out of distance the opponent's trunk can be touched by taking a step forward and lunging, and his arm by lunging directly. From correct distance the adversary's torso can be hit by lunging, and his arm by remaining in the guard position. From close distance the opponent's trunk or arm can be reached without lunging.[16]

Menacé *French.* the feint direct (feint by straight thrust).[17]

Mezzo-cerchio (see *demi-cercle*) *old Italian.* parry of half circle now called first.[23]

Molinello (see circular cut) *Italian.* circular cut.[31]

Molinello montante (see ascending cut) *Italian.* the ascending circular cut.[31]

Moulinet (see circular cut) **1.** *French.* the circular cut. **2.** Beke and Polgár[7] state that they consider the cut and parry moulinets (circular cuts and parries) outmoded, and that they have therefore discarded them as obsolete.

Offensive and counteroffensive actions: Foil

1. *French.*

A. Simple attacks: straight thrust, disengagement, cut-over.

B. Compound attacks.

C. Preparations for the attack:

    1. Attacks on the blade: beat, pressure, expulsion.

    2. Takings of the blade: opposition, bind, *croisé,* envelopment.

    3. Glide.

    4. False attack.

D. Counterattacks: time thrust, arrest, tension.

E. Varieties of attack: redoublement, reprise, remise, countertime.[36]

2. *French.*

A. Simple attacks: straight thrust, disengagement, cut-over, and counter-disengagement.

B. Compound attacks.

C. Preparations for the attack:

    1. Attacks on the blade: beat, pressure, expulsion.

    2. Takings of the blade: opposition, bind, *croisé*, envelopment.

    3. Glide.

    4. False attack.

D. Attacks on the preparation.

E. Counterattacks: arrest, time thrust, attack in the attack.

F. Varieties of attack: redoublement, reprise, remise, countertime.[9]

3. *Italian.*

A. Simple attacks: straight thrust, glide, disengagement, cut-over.

B. Compound attacks:

    1. Feints in opposition to:

        a) simple parries;

        b) circular parries.

    2. Actions on the blade: transports, blade cover, pressures, changes of engagement, beats (simple and change), expulsions (simple and change), disarmaments (spiral right, spiral left, and vertical).

    3. Renewed attack executed from the lunge in opposition to a delayed riposte and by disengagement or with feints.

C. Second intention.

D. Counterattacks: arrest (simple or with a feint), appuntata, disengagement in time, inquartata, passata sotto, time thrust.

E. Countertime: inquartata, passata sotto, and time thrust used in opposition to counterattacks.[26]

4. *Italian.*
   A. Simple attacks: straight thrust, disengagement, glide, cut-over.
   B. Compound attacks:
     1. Feints in opposition to:
       a) simple parries;
       b) circular parries.
     2. Actions on the blade: blade seizure, changes of engagement, transports, envelopments, beats (simple, change, circular, grazing), expulsions, pressures, blade cover, disarmaments (vertical, spiral left, spiral right).
     3. Renewed attack executed in opposition to a delayed riposte:
       a) from the lunge by disengagement;
       b) with a second lunge and by disengagement or with feints;
       c) with an advance lunge and by disengagement or with feints.
   C. Counterattacks: arrest, disengagement in time, appuntata, imbroccata, inquartata, passata sotto, time thrust.
   D. Contraries: countertime (with a parry riposte or a counterattack), feint in time, arrest in countertime.
   E. Attacks in time (including the counter-disengagement).
   F. Second intention.[16]

Offensive and counteroffensive actions: Sabre

1. *Hungarian.*
   A. Simple attacks: direct cuts, point thrust, disengagement with the cut or point thrust, descending cut, and direct cuts to the hand and arm.
   B. Actions on the blade: binds (direct, semicircular, circular, change), beats (direct, semicircular, circular, change).
   C. Feint attacks: single and double.
   D. Counterattacks: disengagement in time with cut or thrust, time cut, arrest with the point.
   E. Second intention, feint in time, arrest in countertime.[24]

2. *Italian.*
   A. Simple attacks: direct point thrust, disengagement with the point, glide with the point, direct cuts, circular cuts, descending cuts.
   B. Compound attacks:
     1. Feints in opposition to:
       a) simple parries;
       b) circular parries.

2. Actions on the blade: blade seizure, changes of engagement, transports, beats (simple, change, circular, grazing), expulsions, pressures.
3. Renewed attack executed:
   a) from the lunge by disengagement with the point or by circular or descending cut;
   b) with a second lunge and by disengagement with the point or by circular or descending cut or with feints;
   c) with an advance lunge and by disengagement with the point or by circular or descending cut or with feints.
C. Counterattacks: arrest, disengagement in time, time thrust or cut to the arm, appuntata, inquartata, time thrust.
D. Contraries: countertime (with a parry riposte or a counterattack), feint in time, arrest in countertime.
E. Attacks in time.
F. Second intention.[16]

Offensive and counteroffensive actions: Épée

1. *French.* offensive and counteroffensive actions in épée are basically those used in foil, but the cut-over should be avoided, and opportunities for employing the counter-disengagement are limited. The counterattacks in épée include the arrest with reassemblement, inquartata, and passata sotto. These last two actions, however, are no longer in use.[9]
2. *Italian.* offensive and counteroffensive actions in épée are essentially the same as in foil fencing except that in the simple attacks the cut-over is replaced with the angulation, in the renewed attacks the second thrust delivered from the lunge is commonly used, in the counterattacks the arrest with reassemblement is most frequently employed, and of the contraries countertime plays an especially important role.[16]

Opposition *(opposition)* **1.** *French.* the taking of the blade with opposition is a progressive opposition in the line of engagement, or following engagement, which continues right up to the end of the attack.[36] **2.** *French.* a sort of pressure executed with the strong of the blade on the weak of the adverse steel, in a progressive and uninterrupted fashion, right up to the completion of the attack.[9]

Opposition of the hand 1. *French.* when the hand is carried to the right.[8]
2. *Italian.* the angle formed by the arm and the weapon, with the vertex at the hand. Opposition has the effect of deviating the adversary's blade,

forcing it in a divergent or oblique direction in respect to the intended line of attack.[32] **3.** *Italian.* with the thrust the hand is shifted progressively to the right or left, depending upon the line of entry. These displacements of the hand are called oppositions, and their function is to provide protection by closing the line.[16]

Parry 1. *French.* the action of turning away, from one's body, the hostile steel. Parries may be simple, half circular, or circular, and these can be executed with opposition or as a beat.[20] **2.** *French.* an action that one employs with one's own weapon to deflect the incoming opposing steel. There are two kinds of parries: the direct, and the circular parry, and these may be executed with opposition or as a beat.[36] **3.** *Hungarian.* the foundation of defense. Its function is to deflect the adversary's blade from our line. There are simple, circular, half circular, and diagonal parries. These may be executed with opposition or a beat.[6] **4.** *Hungarian.* an action which deflects an attacking blade from the target at the exact moment and with a sudden but sure movement of either the medium or the strong of the blade. Parries can be classified in terms of duration, the longer ones being called opposition parries and the shorter ones, beat parries Parries can be categorized by distance covered and method of execution as: simple parries, semicircular parries, diagonal parries, circular parries, and ceding parries.[24] **5.** *Italian.* the action of deviating the adversary's steel during the attack, or avoiding it by withdrawing the body. Parries with the weapon are divided into simple, counter, and half counter parries, and these are subdivided into simple, counter, and half counter parries executed in opposition or with a beat.[32] **6.** *Italian.* a defense of the steel (as opposed to the defense of the measure). It deviates the adversary's blade the moment before it reaches its destination. There are four kinds of parries: simple, counter, half counter, and ceding. Parries can be executed in two diverse ways: by opposition, or with a beat. In the first case, at the conclusion of the parry, the blades are in contact, in the second, they are neatly separated.[30] **7.** *Italian.* defensive movements of the blade that deflect the incoming steel. These can be simple, circular, half circular, or ceding. Simple, circular, and half circular parries may be executed either as opposition or beating motions; ceding parries can only be performed through opposition. In the one instance the adversary's steel is deviated merely by closing the line; in the other it is deflected by striking it to one side.[16]

Parts of the weapon: Foil 1. *French.* the French foil is divided into two principal parts: the blade and the guard. The blade is made of steel and has a strong part near the guard, and a weak part. The guard comprises the grip, bell guard, which protects the hand, and pommel, which permits the assembly of the several parts and acts as a counterbalance. The foil blade is quadrangular and terminates with a button.[36] **2.** *Hungarian.* composed of: the blade, the guard, the grip or handle, and the pommel or locking nut.[24] **3.** *Italian.* the Italian foil is composed of the guard and the blade. The guard serves to protect the hand and consists of the bell guard, cushion, crossbar, arches, handle, and pommel. The blade is made of tempered steel, rectangular in section, and has a button, ricasso, and tang. The blade is divided into three equal parts or gradations: strong, near the bell guard, weak, near the point, and medium or middle between the other two parts.[30]

Parts of the weapon: Sabre 1. *Hungarian.* made up of the blade, the guard, the handle and the locking nut or pommel. The blade, which narrows along its length from the guard to the point, is divided theoretically into three sections: the strong, the middle and the weak. The edge, the back, and the point are also seen as distinct parts. The strong is used for parrying, the middle for making contact by beat or bind with the opponent's blade and the weak for cutting. The point of the blade is used for thrusting. Parries are executed with the edge, while beats and binds can be done with the weak and back of the blade. The guard, as the name suggests, protects the fencer's hand. The handle, usually made of wood, fits on the thick end of the blade. The guard, handle and blade are held together by the locking nut.[24] **2.** *Italian.* divided into two major parts: the guard, and the blade. The guard is comprised of four elements: guard, cushion, grip, and nut. The blade consists of seven elements: blunted end, counter-cut, back, cut, grooves, heel, and tang. Degrees of strength are distinguished by dividing the blade into three equal sections: strong, medium, and weak.[16]

Passata sotto a counterattack against both simple and compound attacks ending in the outside high line. From an invitation or engagement in second (French *octave*) or fourth (French *quarte*), the attack with a straight thrust or disengagement to the high line, or outside high line, is opposed with the counterthrust to the low line, hand in second position (pronation), opposition to the right, left leg extended along the line of direction, and body lowered, with the chest close to the right thigh, and left hand resting on the floor near the right foot. Against a compound attack, the counterattack follows a parry.[16]

Placements of the weapon the positions assumed by the fencer with his armed hand when standing on guard in front of his adversary. The three placements are invitation, engagement, and weapon or blade in line.[30]

Positions there are only three positions: that which one takes before assuming the guard position; the guard position; and the lunge.[33]

Pressure 1. *French.* the action of pressing upon the opponent's blade in order to deflect it or to obtain a reaction from it.[12] **2.** *Italian.* a gradual application of force with the strong or medium of the blade against the adversary's weak to deviate it from its position in line. Like a beat, the pressure is identified by the line in which it encounters the opposing steel: first or half circle, second, third, and fourth.[16]

Prise de fer *French.* designates the group of actions that take the opponent's blade: *opposition, liement, croisé,* and *enveloppement.*[36]

Probing actions (see false attacks) *Italian.* feigned attacks that test the adversary's defensive and counteroffensive responses. His reactions to simulated assaults with feints and beats will indicate whether he defends himself with simple or circular parries, or, instead, has a tendency to counterattack.[16]

Pronation the position of the hand when the fingernails are turned toward the earth. Its opposite is supination.[33]

Quarte sur les armes the old French parry now called *sixte.*[8]

Raddoppio (see gaining on the lunge).

Reassemblement (see also *riunita*) *French.* the action of quitting the guard position to reassume first position.[37]

Redoublement **1.** *French.* same as *reprise;* it is the immediate delivery of a second thrust, without rising from the lunge, after an attack has been parried. It is never made in the same line in which the attack terminated.[17] **2.** *French.* the action of performing a second attack, immediately after the first, in the same line or in another. Its aim is to profit from the effect produced on the adversary, who, shaken by the first attack, has parried without riposting, or has avoided the thrust by retreating. In the first case, the second attack is preceded by a return backward to the guard, and in the second, by a return forward to the guard.[36] **3.** *French.* a renewal of the attack while on the lunge. It is executed against an opponent who parries and delays his riposte. It can be direct, indirect, or compound.[12] **4.** *French.* consists of executing a second attack after returning on guard either forward or backward, against an adversary, who, shaken by the first action, has parried without riposting, or has retreated from the attack.[9]

Remise (also see appuntata) **1.** *French.* a time thrust on the riposte; it is the action of placing the point on the body, without rising from the lunge, and during the adversary's riposte or preparation for the riposte. It is determined by the hesitation of the defender, or by the movement that follows his parry, while the *redoublement* is motivated by the immobility of the defender. The *remise* is calculated; the *redoublement* comes from inspiration. The *remise* is nearly always made with a straight thrust; the *redoublement* is nearly always made by disengagement or cut-over.[17] **2.** *French.* consists of placing the point of the weapon by means of a straight thrust on the adversary's body on the same side as the parry.[10] **3.** *French.* a time thrust executed from the lunge in opposition to the adversary's compound riposte.[36] **4.** *French.* the replacing of the point on the target, while on the lunge, in the line in which the attack has been parried, and must not comprise an additional blade or arm movement. It is executed against an opponent who, parries incompletely and fails to riposte, parries and delays his riposte, parries and uses an indirect or compound riposte. To be valid, it must arrive one movement ahead of the final movement of the riposte.[12] **5.** *French.* always executed with a straight thrust, and without withdrawing the arm, in opposition to an adversary who, after having parried, leaves the blade, or ripostes indirectly or with a feint.[9]

Renewed attacks (*ripigliata* or *ripresa di attacco*) **1.** *Hungarian.* can be executed when the opponent: parries the original attack but delays his riposte or fails to riposte; parries the original attack but retreats instead of making a riposte; or withdraws in the face of the attack either with or without parrying. They differ from initial attacks in several technical aspects. They start from the lunge and not the on-guard position, and the arm is extended, not bent when the movement is begun. The footwork which accompanies renewed attacks includes: the lengthening of the lunge when the opponent has parried in place or with a short step backward (close distance in terms of renewed attacks); renewing the lunge by bringing up the rear foot, or continuing with a *flèche* from the lunge when the opponent retreats without making a riposte (medium distance in terms of renewed attacks); closing distance with a step or jump forward after a forward recovery to on-guard position followed by lunge or *flèche* when the opponent retreats a great distance (long distance in terms of renewed attacks). If a feint attack is applied as a renewed attack, only a simple single feint attack introduced by a disengagement should be used.[24] **2.** *Italian.* the *raddoppio dritto* and *raddoppio cavando:* When the adversary, instead of parrying with his blade, escapes the thrust by retreating out of distance, or better, by using the defense of measure, you return on guard by bringing the left foot forward to regain correct lunging distance, and then execute a straight thrust. If, however, the opponent is not content with only the defense of measure, but unites this with a parry, you employ the same renewed attack, not with a straight thrust, but with a disengagement.[15] **3.** *Italian.* it occurs sometimes that the adversary, instead of parrying your thrust, uses the defense of measure, and with a step or jump backward, takes himself out of distance; therefore, from the lunge itself, you repeat the action, returning on guard with the left leg, and then lunging immediately with the right. The renewed attack *(raddoppio)* can be executed with every kind of attack.[14] **4.** *Italian.* nothing other than a second offensive action initiated from the lunge, that is, immediately after the first attack fails, and is rendered possible by the adversary's failure to react after having defended himself. The new action must therefore be executed in opposition to the blade placement the opponent maintained or assumed in defending himself, and according to the distance established immediately after the attack. It can be used against the adversary who, having regularly parried the attack, lingers or does not riposte at all. In this case one remains in the lunge position and with an appel directs the new thrust to the target area opposite the parry the antagonist used to defend himself with. This is called the second thrust. The opponent can parry with a step backward, in which case it is opportune to return on guard with the left foot, and without pause, to deliver a new thrust with a lunge. This can be accomplished also with a feint or double feint, or with an action on the blade if, on retreating, the antagonist places his weapon in line. The action, coordinated in this way, is called a renewed attack with lunge. And if the opponent employs the defense of measure, retreating further than is necessary, the return on guard is again with the left foot, and a new offensive action is launched in opposition to the adversary's placement of his blade, with a step forward and lunge. This action is called a renewed attack with an advance. The renewed attack can also be executed by gaining on the lunge or with a running attack effected directly from the lunge, or after returning forward on guard.[30]   **5.** *Italian.* second offensive actions launched against an opponent who, having parried the initial assault, either hesitates or fails to respond. The second thrust is executed in opposition to the placement of the adversary's weapon at the completion of the parry. Depending upon fencing measure, renewed attacks may be effected from the lunge, with a second lunge, or with a step forward and lunge. If the opponent parries from a stationary position, the renewed assault is accomplished from the lunge with an appel, and second thrust to the target area opposite the line in which the original attack was parried; if he retreats with his parry, the renewed assault is performed by recovering forward to the guard position, and then attacking with a second lunge; and if, after parrying, he uses the defense of measure, and steps out of distance, the renewed attack is made by recovering forward to the guard position, and then attacking with a step forward and lunge. Renewed attacks can also be effected by gaining on the lunge, or with a running attack, directly from the lunge, or after resuming the guard position with the left foot. When the second thrust is executed from the lunge it is called a replacement.[16]

Reprise **1.** *French.* an offensive action executed, without rising from the lunge, after the adversary parries but does not riposte.[36]   **2.** *French.* a renewal of attack preceded by a return to guard, either backward or forward. It is executed against an opponent who, parries and fails to riposte, parries and retreats while failing to riposte. It can be simple or compound.[12]   **3.** *French.* consists of renewing the attack from the lunge, after withdrawing the arm, in opposition to an adversary who parries and neither ripostes nor retreats. The action can be executed with a straight thrust, by disengagement, cut-over, and counter-disengagement, or it can be preceded by an action on the blade. It can also be performed after a riposte (or counter-riposte) when the adversary has parried without counter-riposting.[9]

Retreat **1.** *French.* made to take oneself out of fencing measure and to parry a surprise attack.[20]   **2.** *French.* the action of moving away from the adversary in order to be outside his range of attack.[37] **3.** *Italian.* the step back serves to gain distance for a respite when the adversary comes too close.[30] **4.** *Italian.* a step backward to increase measure between oneself and the opponent. This motion is also called breaking ground.[16]

Riposte 1. *French.* the attack that follows the parry. It may be immediate *(tac au tac)* or delayed *(à temps perdu).* The compound riposte must never go beyond two movements, the feint and the thrust.[17] **2.** *French.* the thrust delivered after the parry, with or without a lunge. It is called direct when it is executed in the line in which the parry was taken, compound in a contrary case, and *tac au tac* or *à temps perdu,* depending upon whether or not it was immediate.[36] **3.** *French.* the thrust performed after the parry. It may be executed in place, with an advance, a retreat, a lunge, or a *flèche.* One distinguishes two categories of ripostes: simple and compound. Simple ripostes are direct when they are executed in the same line as the parry, and indirect when they are performed in an opposite line. Compound ripostes are those preceded by one or more feints: one-two, double, cut-over-disengage, etc. The riposte may be made in two ways: *tac au tac* or opposition. Finally, all ripostes changing the line (indirect or compound) can be made *à temps perdu,* that is to say, without immediately following the parry.[9] **4.** *German.* the thrust after the parry. There are several kinds of ripostes: simple direct, simple indirect, and compound. The defender may also, on tactical grounds, wish to delay the riposte.[21] **5.** *Hungarian.* the thrust that follows the parry. It is simple or compound and may be executed with opposition, as a beat, or with delay.[6] **6.** *Italian.* the thrust that is delivered to the adversary after the parry. When the riposte is effected in one movement it is called simple, and may be accomplished by detaching the blade or by maintaining contact *(filo).*[28] **7.** *Italian.* the thrust delivered immediately after the adversary's offensive action is parried is designated the riposte. It can be simple or compound, and may be performed by detaching the blade (straight thrust), or by maintaining contact with the adverse steel (glide). If a disengagement is added to the simple riposte to elude the counterparry of the adversary, it is called a riposte with feint.[30] **8.** *Italian.* the thrust delivered immediately after the adversary's attack has been parried. It may be simple or compound. Opposition parries can be followed by ripostes in which the blade is detached (straight thrust), or kept in contact (glide). Ripostes consisting of two or more blade motions are termed compound ripostes; their function is to elude one or more counterparries, that is, parries opposed to the riposte.[16]

Riunita (see arrest with reassemblement). *Italian.* reassemblement.

Running attack (see *flèche*) a rapid advance with the left foot passing the right.[16]

Salute a traditional act of courtesy directed to the adversary and spectators, and must always be observed at the beginning and end of the lesson and combat.[16]

Scandaglio (see probing actions).

Second intention 1. *Hungarian.* a movement executed against a habitual action of the opponent, such as a tendency to riposte to the same target area, or against an action induced or deduced in advance, such as a planned counterattack by the opponent.[24] **2.** *Italian.* the movement is performed with the express purpose of provoking defensive responses against which counteractions can be applied. It is especially useful in opposition to the adversary who, following a particular parry, always ripostes in the same line. The distinction between second intention and countertime is that second intention prompts a parry and riposte which is opposed with the counterparry and riposte, while countertime provokes a counterattack which is countered with the parry and riposte, or with another counterattack.[16]

Septime haute (see *demi-cercle* and *mezzo-cerchio*) *old French.* parry of half circle or high seventh, which was used to protect the inside high line.[17]

Simple attacks: Foil 1. *French.* the weapon makes the minimum movement necessary to direct the point to the body; it does not allow for a feint; it is the attack reduced to its most simple expression; and it consists of a single tempo in which the point is directed to the body of the adversary in an uncovered line. It is made with the straight thrust, disengagement, and the cut-over.[17] **2.** *French.* those which are not preceded by a feint. These are the straight thrusts, disengagements, cut-overs, and counter-disengagements.[33] **3.** *French.* actions that are effected in one tempo in which the extension of the arm is coordinated with the lunge (or *flèche*). There are four different forms: the straight thrust, the disengagement, the cut-over, and the counter-disengagement.[9] **4.** *German.* it requires only one movement, and scores a hit via the shortest route. The simple attacks are: the straight thrust, the disengagement, and the cut-over.[21] **5.** *Hungarian.* performed with only one movement. It may be executed in three ways: with the straight thrust, the disengagement, and the cut-over. To these simple attacks must also be added the counter-disengagement, which we effect on the adversary's movement.[6] **6.** *Italian.* those that consist of a single movement. These comprise the straight thrust, disengagement, and glide.[15] **7.** *Italian.* those executed without the intention of eluding a parry: the straight thrust, glide, disengagement, and cut-over.[25] **8.** *Italian.* all offensive actions which are developed without eluding the adversary's parry. These are the straight thrust, disengagement, glide and flanconade in fourth, and simple beat and straight thrust.[30] **9.** *Italian.* offensive actions consisting of a single blade movement. In foil fencing there are four simple attacks: the straight thrust, the disengagement, the glide and flanconade in fourth, and the cut-over.[16]

Simple beat effected by moving the blade the shortest distance necessary to encounter the opposing steel. It may be executed from an invitation or engagement; the engagement can be one's own or the adversary's. In the latter case the beat is called a false beat.[16]

Simple parries: Foil **1.** *French.* those that travel directly to the line of attack. There are eight, two for each line: first *(prime)*, second *(seconde)*, third *(tierce)*, fourth *(quarte)*, fifth *(quinte)*, sixth *(sixte)*, seventh *(septime)*, and eighth *(octave)*. The simple parries for the high lines are third, fourth, fifth, sixth; and the simple parries for the low lines are first, second, seventh, and eighth. In the parries of first, second, third, and fifth the hand is placed in pronation; and in the parries of fourth, sixth, seventh, and eighth the hand is placed in supination. Gomard was the first to give the eight parries their numerical name.[33] **2.** *French.* the action made by the defender in carrying his sword arm and sword across the body in order to oppose his strong to the attacking weak with the purpose of deflecting it. The hand is placed in a half supinated position in both fourth and sixth. Pronated parries have disappeared, or are being less used. Fifth, which is nothing more than a bad fourth, has been banished by most masters, as has been third. Octave, executed in the low line in the same manner as its brother sixth in the high line, has replaced the parry of second. In brief, sounder basic parries have simplified the defense.[12] **3.** *Hungarian.* two pairs of parries protect the fencing target against attacks to the upper area and two protect the lower target areas. The fourth, sixth, eighth and seventh parries are executed with the hand in a supine position. For fifth, third, second and first parries, the hand is held in a prone position. The high sixth and seventh combination used to parry cut-overs is executed with the hand in a prone position. Whether the hand is held in supine or prone position, the parry must deflect the attack with the edge of the blade.[24] **4.** *Italian.* there are four simple parries executed in opposition or with a beat, each having its own corresponding line of defense: the parry of fourth *(quarta)* protects the inside high line; the parry of third *(terza),* the outside high line; the parry of second *(seconda),* the inside and outside low lines; and the parry of half circle *(mezzocerchio* or modern Italian first), the high and low lines.[32] **5.** *Italian.* protective displacements of the blade that cover exposed target areas by traveling the shortest route from one invitation or engagement to another. In foil fencing there are four, each defending a certain portion or portions of the valid target: thus, the parry of first or half circle protects the inside high and low lines, the parry of second, the outside low line, the parry of third, the outside high line, and the parry of fourth, the inside high line. Placement of the arm, hand, and weapon is the same as in invitations and engagements designated by the same number. When the parrying action is correctly executed, the strong of the defending blade encounters the medium of the attacking steel.[16]

Simple parries: Sabre 1. *Hungarian.* both the point and guard move from one position to another along the shortest possible route in either a horizontal or vertical plane. Five parries, corresponding to the five invitations, are taught in sabre fencing. They are first, second, third, fourth and fifth parries.[24] **2.** *Italian.* there are six simple parries, each covering certain parts of the valid target: thus, the parry of first protects the left cheek, inside chest, abdomen, and internal arm; the parry of second, the flank, and bottom of arm; the parry of third, the right cheek, outside chest, flank, and external arm; the parry of fourth, the left cheek, inside chest, abdomen, and internal arm; the parry of fifth, the head, and top of arm; and the parry of sixth, the head, and top of arm. Placement of the hand and weapon is the same as in invitations and engagements designated by the same number. In the past there were also parries of low third and low fourth. These are nothing more than lowered parries of third and fourth which serve as alternate parries for second and first to defend, respectively, the flank and abdomen.[16]

Simple ripostes 1. *French.* are direct when they are executed in the same line as the parry (sixth-direct, fourth-direct); and they are said to be indirect when they are performed in a line adjoining that of the parry (disengagement, cut-over, and counter-disengagement). All ripostes that change lines may be made *à temps perdu.*[9] **2.** *Hungarian.* may be direct or indirect. The direct simple riposte is executed in the same line as the parry; the simple indirect riposte is performed in a line other than that of the parry.[6] **3.** *Italian.* the riposte in one movement.[28]

Spada nera *old Italian.* name for the practice rapier.[25]

Spade di marra practice rapiers; these were replaced by foils.[25]

Stop-hit (see arrest).

Straight thrust: Foil 1. *French.* the action of directing the point to the body in a straight line; it is the movement in which all thrusts terminate.[17] **2.** *French.* its name alone serves to define it. It is the result of driving the weapon along the most direct route.[20] **3.** *French.* the action of directing the point to the body, without changing the line, extending the arm, and lunging.[33] **4.** *French.* an action executed in the line of engagement left open by the adversary.[36] **5.** *German.* the most simple form of attack, and is executed in one tempo. It follows the shortest and most direct path to the adversary's target.[21] **6.** *German.* the most simple of all attacks. In this the point of the blade, without interference (of the adversary's arm or weapon), can reach, via the shortest path, the opponent's target area.[5] **7.** *Hungarian.* among attacks the most simple. The point of the weapon moves forward in a straight line, followed by a harmonious movement of our body.[6] **8.** *Italian.* thrust delivered in such a way that the blade does not slide or glide along that of the adversary. This is the most simple action of attack, and occupies the first place of importance in fencing with the point. All offensive actions must of necessity terminate in the straight thrust. The straight thrust may be executed from one's own four engagements, or, having the weapon in line, on the adversary's invitation.[32] **9.** *Italian.* an action, without blade contact, in which the point of the weapon follows a straight line to the exposed target; it is a direct attack in one movement, and may be used when the adversary makes an invitation, or from one's own invitation or engagement.[16]

Supination the position of the hand when the fingernails are turned toward the sky. Its opposite is pronation.[33]

Temps perdu *French.* a delayed riposte.[9]

Tension *French.* the extension of the arm on the adversary's attack.[33]

Thrust in low fourth *(quarta bassa)* *Italian.* an auxiliary action. It is a simple attack executed in one motion against the antagonist who exposes his low line by habitually keeping his hand high in the invitation, engagement, or parry of fourth. Instead of directing the thrust to the outside high line, it is aimed at the low line, with the hand in fourth position.[16]

Time 1. *Italian.* that favorable instant taken by the fencer to attack his adversary while he is distracted, or when he makes an incorrect movement which exposes some part of the body.[23] **2.** *Italian.* favorable moment at which an offensive action will catch the adversary off guard.[16]

Time-hit (see time thrust).

Time thrust 1. *French.* an action opposed to the adversary's attack. It ordinarily consists of a single movement, and must be taken with opposition so that one is protected against the hostile steel.[17] **2.** *French.* an attack with opposition against a compound attack, intercepting the line where the adversary's final action will terminate.[33] **3.** *French.* a time-hit (time thrust) is a stop-hit (arrest) which anticipates, and intercepts, the final line of attack, and is delivered in such a way that the executant is covered.[12] **4.** *Italian.* a counterattack that precedes the final movement of the attack. It is directed in the same line as the assault, with exactly enough opposition to deviate the incoming steel.[16]

Traccheggio (see actions of concealment).

Transports (see bind) *Italian.* changes of line effected from an engagement or parry without losing contact with the hostile steel, but dominating it as the line is changed. There are four transports: the transport from third to half circle (first) or the internal flanconade; the transport from fourth to second or the flanconade in second; the transport from second to fourth; and the transport from half circle (first) to third.[32]

Triple feint eludes three parries; they are opposed to the invitation and engagement. The feints may be coordinated with an advance. The first feint is made with the motion of the right foot, the second with the movement of the left foot, the third from immobility, and the final thrust with the lunge.[16]

Trompment Crosnier[12] states that *tromper* is to deceive. A *trompment* is therefore a deception. In fencing it is a term used to describe the blade actions which deceive an opponent's parry.

Varieties of attack *(variétés d'attaques)* the French category of actions: *redoublement, reprise, remise,* and *contre-temps.*[9]

Velocity the minimum time necessary to complete an offensive, defensive, or counteroffensive movement.[16]

Volte (also see inquartata) *French.* an action that carries the body to the right or left by pivoting on the right foot.[33]

Warde in the English publication, *Di Grassi his true Arte of Defence* (1594), used to designate a guard or parry position.

Bibliography

1. Alajmo, Michele. *Come si diventa spadisti.* Rodi, 1936.
2. Barbasetti, Luigi. *La scherma di spada.* Milano, 1902.
3. *The Art of the Foil.* New York, 1932.
4. ————, *The Art of the Sabre and the Épée.* New York, 1936.
5. Barth, Berndt. *Fechten.* Berlin, 1979.
6. Bay, Rerrich, Tilli. *Florett und Degenfechten.* Berlin, 1956.
7. Beke, Zoltán, and Polgár, Jozsef. *The Methodology of Sabre Fencing.* Budapest, 1963.
8. Boëssière, (M. La). *Traité de l'art des armes.* Paris, 1818.
9. Cléry, Raoul. *L'escrime.* Paris, 1973.
10. Cordelois. *Leçons d'armes.* Paris, 1862.
11. Crosnier, Roger. *Fencing with the Épée.* London, n.d.
12. ————, *Fencing with the Foil.* London, 1968.
13. ————, *Fencing with the Sabre.* London, n.d.
14. Enrichetti, Cesare. *Trattato elementare teorico-pratico di scherma.* Parma, 1871.
15. Florio, Blasco. *La scienza della scherma.* Catania, 1844.
16. Gaugler, William. *The Science of Fencing.* Bangor, 1997.
17. Gomard, (A.-J.-J. Posselier). *La theorie de l'escrime.* Paris, 1845.
18. Greco, Agesilao. *La spada e la sua disciplina d'arte.* Roma, 1912.
19. Greco, Aurelio. *La spada e la sua applicazione.* Roma, 1907.
20. Grisier, Augustin. *Les armes et le duel.* Paris, 1847.
21. Kerstenhan, Karl. *Florettfechten.* München, 1978.
22. Lafaugère, Louis-Justin. *Traité de l'art de faire des armes.* Paris, 1825.
23. Lambertini, Vittorio. *Trattato di scherma.* Bologna, 1870.
24. Lukovich, István. *Fencing.* Budapest, 1986.
25. Marchionni, Alberto. *Trattato di scherma.* Firenze, 1847.
26. Masiello, Ferdinando. *La scherma italiana di spada e di sciabola.* Firenze, 1887.

27. Nadi, Aldo. *On Fencing.* New York, 1943; Bangor, 1996.
28. Parise, Masaniello. *Trattato teorico-pratico della scherma di spada e sciabola.* Roma, 1884.
29. Pecoraro, Salvatore, e Pessina, Carlo. *La scherma di sciabola.* Roma, 1910.
30. Pessina, Giorgio, e Pignotti, Ugo. *Il fioretto.* Roma, 1970.
31. ————, *La sciabola.* Roma, 1972.
32. Pini, Eugenio. *Trattato pratico e teorico sulla scherma di spada.* Livorno, 1903.
33. Prévost, Camille. *Théorie pratique de l'escrime.* Paris, 1886.
34. Radaelli, Giuseppe. *Istruzione per la scherma di sciabola e di spada.* Milano, 1876.
35. Rastelli, Giorgio. *La scherma.* Milano, 1942.
36. *Règlement d'escrime 1908.* Paris, 1914.
37. Robert, Georges. *La science des armes.* Paris, 1900.
38. Rondelle, Louis. *Foil and Sabre: A Grammar of Fencing.* Boston, 1892.
39. Rossi, Giordano. *Scherma di spada e sciabola.* Milano, 1885.
40. Scorza, Rosaroll, e Grisetti, Pietro. *La scienza della scherma.* Nocera, 1871.
41. Szabó, László. *Fencing and the Master.* Budapest, 1977.
42. Thirieux, Pierre. *Escrime moderne.* Paris, 1970.
43. Vass, Imre. *Épée Fencing.* Budapest, 1976.

Other Books from Laureate Press